THE CALL WITHIN

The Call Within

From Ordinary to Extraordinary

James Graham Johnston

mse
PRESS

Cover design and watercolor illustration by the author

The Call Within

Second Edition

First Edition 2001 Writers Club Press

Copyright © 2010 James Graham Johnston
All rights reserved.
ISBN: 1451502176
ISBN-13: 9781451502176
For correspondence or permissions, please contact:
jgjohnston@GiftsCompass.com

For Lindsey and Kylee

Contents

Preface

It took a long time to write this short book. It would have been written more quickly if I had not started writing it when I was so far from my own center.

I had much trouble finding my "voice" and writing what I felt to be *true*. Not until it occurred to me that I should write this book as a letter to my daughters—as a summary of what I would want them to know about life should I not be around—did I finally find my voice.

Finding my voice also required finding my own call within. I had found it early in life, then lost it, then through a personal about-face that was about as nimble as turning the Queen Elizabeth around, I found it again.

The many iterations of early drafts of this book would provide a useful overview of that anguished personal process of transformation. Each of the early attempts at a manuscript were themselves anguished and clumsy. My wife, Chris, patiently read and insightfully critiqued them all.

Later, when I started to find my voice, Lynn Stratton provided much helpful guidance in matters of word choice and grammatical structure. She edited the first edition, published in 2001. For this second edition, Judy Ludwig provided a very thorough, precise, and thought-provoking editorial review. If a point is well made or an insight well-spoken, either Judy or Lynn deserve much of the credit.

In the nine-year interim between the first and second editions, I became well acquainted with the psychology of Carl Jung and the philosophy of Quaker mystic, Rufus Jones. They affirmed, each with his particular framework, that the way of the spirit is real and of utmost importance in human experience. Their enormous bodies of work enabled me to more confidently produce this small edition.

Early in the journey of my life, I awoke amidst the noisy streets and quiet ruins of Rome where the trusted way was lost. I was fortunate to meet Richard Callner, the director of the school of art where I was enrolled. He became a compassionate guide for me; if I had not known him, I might have gone back to sleep.

I am indebted to each of these people, and to many others, who have immeasurably contributed to my life, to my understanding of what is most vitally important, and therefore, to this book.

Go confidently in the direction of your dreams. Live the life you have imagined.

Thoreau

Chapter One

Awakening to the Call

There are only two ways to live your life. One is as though nothing is a miracle. The other is as though everything is a miracle.

Albert Einstein

We live on a planet in a seemingly isolated corner of the universe. We neither know for certain how we got here nor what the future holds. Our world is held by a mysterious force that keeps us on track, poised and balanced with other colossal orbs, as we hurl concentrically around a blazing sun. Despite our restricted understanding of this force, we have given it a name: *gravity*.

Giving a mysterious phenomenon a name downgrades the nature of the mystery, pigeonholing it in a mental compartment that we might call "the known." Considering the wondrous to be *known* alters our perception of it. It cheapens the phenomenon, makes it ordinary, and dulls our sense of wonder. It leads us to believe that the miraculous is not truly wondrous at all.

No one really understands how or why gravity occurs, yet it is considered known nevertheless. When the mysteries of life are superficially categorized this way, a grand charade begins that renders the wondrous ordinary. In the same way, if we characterize the miracle of our own lives by some narrow and constricting self-concept, we, too, debase the wondrous and render it ordinary.

When I attended university as a young man, I used to walk to a vast cornfield at sunset to watch the sun sink beneath the horizon. It was a daily pilgrimage for me, a tribute to an astonishing event. I could almost feel the earth turn as the sun left my view. All of life seemed a great miracle, and I felt fortunate to be alive to experience it.

I have too often forgotten to take that pilgrimage as I have matured. Forgotten? Well, not exactly.

Most often I have just been "too busy." I have been besieged by the tyranny of what appeared to be "urgent."

As our lives become more complicated, we often tend to have better things to do than to make pilgrimages to open fields. We have places to go and appointments to keep. There is just a lot of "stuff" to "get done." If there aren't critically important meetings to attend, then there are vitally important errands to run. The paper must be read, the money earned, the bills paid, the deal done, the promotion obtained, the calendar filled, the career established, the influence gained, the toys accumulated, the goals accomplished. The dizzying, ordinary, obsessive play must go on, and there is little time for wondering about the miraculous.

Yet, if we do not take the time to connect to the wondrous, to the beautiful, to the true and the good, our lives become flat and one-dimensional. Life hardly seems worth living. We lose the inspiration, the passion, and the enthusiasm that normally sustain us. We lose our grasp of the immense phenomenon of *life* and its staggering, relentless movement through time.

Pause for a moment to see life in this world from a larger perspective. In your imagination step beyond our world, as though you were stepping into the black unknown of space. Now imagine turning to look back. Can you see our world? Do you see the ethereal clouds, the deep blue oceans, and the green and terra-cotta land masses? Our planet is fresh and alive—a marvel of color and life against the black unknown. There is some inconceivable, breathtaking miracle at work on this floating globe, suspended in the heavens by seemingly nothing—a miracle in which we are all participants.

From this larger perspective, you may begin to get a hint of an extraordinary, inexpressible purpose underway here. There is a momentous story unfolding on this world, a drama of growth and evolution toward some awesome destiny that cannot quite be touched or seen. Every creature and every particle of every atom perform their roles in this celestial theater of *life* marching through time.

Consider the possibility that you were placed in this world to play a significant part in that drama of life, that you, too, are here to begin a special purpose. Consider that your contribution is important and meaningful for the outworking of the universal mystery underway. Consider that what you do and how you live your life *matters*, and that it matters not just to the people you encounter from day to day, but that it matters to *life*. Consider that your existence here has a purpose that is being silently but surely called forth into this remarkable theater.

I am not talking about a purpose you may have grown accustomed to, an *ordinary one*, one that may have stealthily asserted itself, one that may have you caught up in the bustle of daily routine or one that defines you as some mechanical cog in social machinery. I am not referring to the one that may demean your life and your sense of calling, nor the one that says you should do what everyone else does and strive for the things everyone else wants, nor the one that has you inextricably bound to the culture you live in, nor the one that keeps you from being the individual you were created to be.

I'm talking about a different one—*the other one*.

Consider that there is another purpose, one that you carry within you, one that has an *extraordinary* quality about it, one imbued with a faint but compelling luminosity, one you may keep suppressed for fear of what may happen if you let it out, one that might call you to some noble purpose. *That one*. The one that would take all the courage you can muster.

The one that is not common yet feels more natural than anything you have ever known.

That one.

What is that special purpose for which you were created? What is the calling that would consume your life and demand your highest integrity? Seek it, and out of the mystery of life, it will be *given* to you.

In that quiet, sacred place known as the "inner life," your calling awaits. It is known by many names: *passion, dream, vision, purpose, vocation, mission*. These words all attempt to articulate what can never be adequately described—a unique destiny that quietly lures you like an ancient siren and begs to be discovered.

Discover Your Call

Sometimes the journey of discovery seems direct and clear. Some people know very early what they want to do in life. At the age of eight, they may say, "I want to be a doctor," and then they spend the rest of their lives becoming and living the lives of doctors. Their calling readily finds expression in their work. Others, though, are given to a long, arduous struggle. Nothing satisfies them for long; they bounce from one pursuit to another. "Dreamers," they are called, or "job-hoppers." Their journey is fraught with frustration, even embarrassment, but the calling lures them on, seeking to be more fully expressed.

A calling often starts as a small hint of an idea, an urging echo of an unlived destiny. It is like the purposeful *élan vital* of an acorn that *must* become a full-grown oak. Unlike the acorn, we have a choice: We can nurture the calling, or we can avoid it. Either way, the calling will have its say. The persistent call within, urging us to our destiny, will not simply vanish because we ignore it. We may grow dull to it, but it is still embedded in the soul. The call will not cease, one way or the other, to make its presence known.

When life is lived as an expression of our call, it produces an abiding anticipation and a peace of mind. It satisfies the urge to be about something significant and to make a difference in some way. We feel that we are on the right course. The calling gathers us up like an ocean swell and delivers us to a coast that feels perpetually new, original, and robust.

A call ignored or demeaned also has its consequences. Life can become dull and hollow. The ocean swell passes and we are left floundering in the ebb of an inauthentic life, safe perhaps temporarily, but not sound. The call will not leave us to our small lives undisturbed. The relentless haunting of an unlived life, dying within us, plagues us everywhere we go. A yawning void gapes ever wider within us and all the trinkets, toys, prestige, or drugs in the world cannot fill that empty chasm.

Sometimes we are afraid to follow a calling, afraid of where it may lead us, and our fears are often well founded. A calling may transport us to a more strenuous life. It may require a great deal of work. Following a calling does not guarantee a life of ease or uninterrupted bliss. The rain will fall on the just and the unjust, the good and the evil, as it has for millennia, but following a calling does provide the assurance of living a *deeper* life, a life that is rooted in the soul. It engenders an abiding joy and feeling of fulfillment.

St. Francis of Assisi was allegedly asked, while tending his garden, what he would do if he learned that he had only a short time to live. He simply replied that he would continue tending his garden. Einstein was still penciling out attempted solutions for a unified field theory—on his deathbed.

A calling becomes the reason for living. It is the *morning star* that orients life's direction. It is the perpetual "place" in life that is constant and dependable. Once found, no other place seems as fulfilling or whole.

Yet following a calling, by definition, means following something beyond your ability to manipulate it, and that can also be threatening. When you are in control of your life, you may readily imagine how things will turn out. You have your bags packed and you know where you are going. You may even think you know when you are going to die, and you may already be planning how to spend your final years. You may have an idea about how you will be living next year (usually very much the way you lived this year). You may think that you can see the end from the beginning. Even if your life has been a miserable failure, you at least know that you will probably continue to fail miserably—*and that can be comforting.* At least there is a sense of predictability about it!

When you follow the morning star of your calling, you cease to be so certain of your future. Each day is a new adventure of discovery, for you have entered into a partnership with what is *real* and beyond you. Your primary role is to have *faith* that you will get the guidance and assistance you need as you progress.

Faith goes against many natural instincts for self-preservation and of the desire of the ego for control. Yet when you step apart from your need to control, you discover a new self that is stronger, more vital, and more committed than the old self ever could be. Pursuing a calling is engaging in a partnership with a venerable inner guide—a "still small voice" within.

Living with faith in that unseen guide may require courageous commitment from you, but the fruits of that courage spur you on. Each day feels more substantial and alive. The calling that started as a vague feeling of a new direction seems to expand and take shape as you pursue it. You discover a growing passion over which you exercise little control—and then you find that you do not want to control it. You do not want to put the fire out!

From Ordinary to Extraordinary

A calling may be very compatible with a common walk of life. It is not what people *do* that makes it extraordinary, but *why* and *how* they do it. As Mother Teresa observed, we can do no extraordinary things, only *ordinary* things with great love. A calling often leads to a life filled with great love—a love for life, a love for work, a love for people—and *that* is what makes it extraordinary.

It is also true that a calling can lead to some remarkable accomplishments. Florence Nightingale, who felt "a call from God to his service" at age eleven, went on to transform deplorable conditions of health care when she founded the profession of nursing.

Anwar Sadat became president of Egypt and courageously pursued unprecedented initiatives for peace with Israel. He found his calling during a period of imprisonment and solitary confinement, about which he wrote, "Once released from the narrow confines of the 'self' . . . a man will have stepped into a new undiscovered world which is vaster and richer . . . I came to experience friendship with God—the only friend who never lets you down or abandons you."

Winston Churchill found a calling in political life, one that dramatically unfolded during the dark days of the Second World War. He wrote of that period, "I felt as if I were walking with destiny, and all my past life had been a preparation for this hour and this trial."

Few of us are called to play such significant roles in history. Yet each of us is *called*. But called to what and to where? Those are the questions for which each of us must find our own answers.

It is not necessary to make a huge contribution to the world. We do not need to win a Nobel Prize or emblazon our names in the book of human history;

but it is necessary to make a contribution. The calling does not urge us to a life of selfish ease. It moves us to effort, to work, to adventure, to exploration, to something beyond our own self-absorption.

It moves us to grow, to become unique individuals, to differentiate ourselves. It moves us to make steady, incremental progress along our journey, to grow in character and in competency. The calling is unfinished music: We hear only the first few bars, and we are called to complete the rest of the opus with our lives.

That composition need not be an epochal, paradigm-shifting symphony. Sometimes the music is just simple, easy, and light.

I remember talking with a young physical education teacher in Denver, Colorado, who was driving a shuttle bus for a rental car company over the summer. She was the happiest, friendliest, most enthusiastic shuttle driver I had ever met. She found humor in everything and took an interest in our lives. By the time we arrived at our destination, we knew her as well as we knew some of our friends, and she knew us. We were family. The mayor and the entire membership of the Denver Chamber of Commerce could not have given us a warmer welcome to the city. She was creating happiness for thousands of people, just by driving a shuttle bus. She may not have been *called* to drive a shuttle bus, but she did seem naturally called to something simple, easy, and light: to bring warmth and friendliness to others.

A young girl, born with a mental disability, had been mainstreamed into a public school. She had been anxious about getting a part in her school play. On the day parts were given out, she came home very excited. "I have a part!" she exclaimed, as she rushed through the front door. "My part is to cheer and clap for all the other children in the play!" Simple, easy, and light.

What is that purpose that calls you to step outside yourself? What brings you joy and enthusiasm? What do you feel passionate about? It may be a political career, or it may be working with three-year-olds in the neighborhood preschool. Maybe it is just to cheer and clap for others. Whatever it is, it can draw you from an ordinary life into an extraordinary one filled with purpose and passion.

Notice the Cues and Clues

How do we find this elusive, invisible calling? Why were we not given an owner's manual for its care or a roadmap for finding our way? In many ways, we have been given both. We will review the owner's manual in chapter 2. The road map, and even the road and all of its directional signs, are often magically right in front of us, day after day, to be noticed or not, depending on the bent of our purposes. If we are attentive, we will find our way.

Each day is full of clues, symbols, signposts, and compass headings we too often miss. When we experience a surge of enthusiasm, are stopped short by an uncanny series of coincidences, or are drawn to a certain passage in a book or line in a movie, our calling may be speaking to us. Life is full of informative cues and clues. It is for us to pay attention, to listen and watch for what they are telling us.

Where do we start? How can we alter our lives to attend to this invisible yet compelling call? Sometimes, we start *right where we are*. Heeding a call often begins by doing what we have already been given to do, *with a whole heart*. "Whatsoever your hand finds to do," wrote the author of Ecclesiastes, "do that with all your heart." The situation we are now in may have been delivered to us as part of the call. It may be cultivating needed growth. If we bring a downcast spirit to our circumstances, we may miss all the inherent value.

Going the extra mile—being willing to do more and to do it more willingly—has a powerful effect, not only on us but also on the people around us. Bringing enthusiasm to life often leads to the next thing—to the next progressive opportunity to discover the life that awaits us. As Martin Luther King, Jr. once recommended, "If you are called to be a street sweeper, sweep the streets as Michelangelo painted . . . Sweep the streets so well that all the hosts of heaven and earth will pause and say, 'Here lived a great sweeper, who did his job well!'"

The way to a calling may also appear as a circuitous path. I spent much of my early life moving from one pursuit to another. I was often terribly frustrated that I couldn't seem to settle on some final career, but my enthusiasm just kept whisking me from one new adventure to another. Just as I was feeling that I was achieving mastery in some work, I would be conveyed to something else.

Now that my calling has become clearer and I am on a steadier, less serpentine journey, I can see the value of almost everything I did and how it can support the life I am choosing. All of those experiences gave me an opportunity to *grow down*, to reach in and experience some aspect of my resources that would not have been developed if I had gone straight to the life I now pursue.

Your calling may arrive early and then consume the rest of your life. It might subtly tap you on the shoulder one day, along the way to doing something else. You may have to struggle and fight to find it. One way or another, if you seek your calling, *it will find you.*

The chief task is to notice when the call arrives. Cues, clues, insights, passions, and epiphanies abound. We seldom notice more than a very slim fraction of those that are given to us, for we tend to relegate them to the *ordinary* experience of life. Among those daily clues are our *interests.*

Trust Your Interests

When we look to the interests that draw our attention, we are seeing the hazy outline of the call. Interests shape the riverbed through which the calling flows. If we try to force a calling to flow outside that riverbed, it can be rough going. We lose energy; everything seems more difficult and forced.

Interests can appear very early in life but can sometimes be smothered by social pressures to do or become something else. An interest may run too much against the grain of family or cultural values. A natural artist born into a conservative family may be encouraged to pursue a "more practical" career. A working-class, patriarchal community may suppress the aspirations of a talented, young male ballet dancer.

Sometimes interests don't fully mature until mid-life. James Michener's interest in writing did not seem to mature until he was about forty, when he wrote his first book. Anna Mary Robertson Moses ("Grandma Moses") did not start painting until she was in her seventies and painted for the remaining years of her long and prolific life. Her paintings were exhibited and bought in galleries around the world, from New York to Tokyo.

People who have pursued their strongest interests have found themselves immersed in projects of service. George Washington Carver pursued his interest in botany and revolutionized agricultural practices. Marie Curie attended to her interest in science and became the first person to be honored with two noble prizes. Margaret Thatcher, a grocer's daughter, followed her interest in politics and became the first female prime minister of Britain.

Interests can also provide balance. You may have to choose which of your interests to include in your work; other interests may need to be pursued more casually. They can provide refreshing respite, helping to keep your career pursuits in a healthy perspective.

Plants naturally turn toward the sun for nourishment. Birds instinctively migrate to beneficial climates. Every cell in your body is "minded" to know its mission and carry it out for the benefit of the whole. By some instinctive consciousness, every living thing seems to *know* what to pursue for its highest well-being. Trust your interests and feed them with your attention. They will do right by you.

Do What You Love

Gifts help to define our unique attributes, and they guide us to our call. Gifts are those natural talents or aptitudes that come easily. With practice or training, they can be developed and refined into specialized skills. An architect, for example, may be a very highly skilled designer, but his skills in architectural design sprang from underlying analytical and aesthetic aptitudes. These underlying gifts were present before the learning began.

We are given gifts for a purpose. If our gifts are discarded or ignored, our inner lives may erupt in frustration and turmoil. A calling invariably uses our best gifts; they abide together like shore to ocean. When we cultivate our gifts, they lead us to a deeper sense of calling; they illuminate the horizons of our individual destinies.

Our best gifts can be oddly elusive; we may blithely take them for granted because they are *too* familiar. They have always been part of our identity, even from early childhood. Like the very air we breathe, they are essential to our well-being, though we may seldom be fully conscious of their value. Some people listen well to others, always willing to "lend an ear," but they would hardly recognize that willingness as a special gift. Yet it *is* a gift, just as the willingness and ability to talk is a gift.

Identifying your best gifts is often a matter of paying attention to what you do naturally and gracefully, virtually without thinking. It consists of simply noticing what you most *enjoy* doing. What is it that you love to do, regardless of whether you are being paid? What brings you "bliss" and invigorates you? Doing what you love fosters your best gifts while orienting you to the course of your unique call.

Revere Your Ideas

Ideas can also be lodestars to the call, leading us to the next step, to the next area of growth. We do not have the power to create ideas nor force them to appear. They are not widgets to be manufactured by us at will. They are *given* to us. They arrive in response to our individual quests and serve us along our way.

When Thomas Edison was involved in his creative struggle to develop a functioning light bulb, he met a problem: The filament burned too quickly and the light bulb would not last. He struggled with this problem, and then after one of his famous twenty-minute naps, awoke with an *idea*. He remembered lying by a fire as a small boy, watching embers smolder in the fireplace. It occurred to him that the embers were smoldering because they were buried—deprived of oxygen. Then he realized that he had the clue that would solve his problem: Remove oxygen from the light bulb! When he created a partial vacuum in the bulb, his problem was solved.

We might call Edison's epiphany a *practical* idea. Practical ideas enable us to negotiate the many daily dilemmas that require practical solutions—the best route to work, the most appropriate birthday gift for a friend, where to buy the food for the evening meal. Practical ideas are an essential part of the process of managing life in the world at large; they are useful and productive. Deep ideas, though, seem to come from somewhere else, someplace, well . . . *deeper*.

Deep ideas resonate. They echo within us. They are imbued with a transcendent quality as they express a deep longing or a call to some noble expression of life. They arrive without warning, often when we least expect them. A deep idea might express itself as a thought like this: *I do not want to die without making a difference in the world.*

Deep ideas may appear as dreams or visions from within. We may see a brief glimpse of an ideal life appearing as a vague inner image, one that shadows our consciousness with its subtle persistence. It hazily delineates a destiny, a way of life that we feel compelled to move toward. These deep ideas are beneficent, intervening thoughts that disturb the clatter of consciousness. They may haunt, jar, disturb, gnaw, and pull at us, but they possess underlying qualities destined for wholeness.

Ideas may also unexpectedly arrive from the world at large. A word or paragraph in a book could inspire us. We could be awed by another's life story. We might admire someone else's commitment and feel motivated to adopt a similar purpose for ourselves. Like the ideas from within, these ideas arriving from experience in the world are also elements of the majestic mystery of life; we must acknowledge them with the reverence they deserve.

Attend to Synchronicities

Modern physics has uncovered some remarkable and unexpected properties of matter that seem to defy conventional assumptions. Matter, at the atomic level, is *not* just mechanical; it is also *relational*. Every atom of every molecule may be connected to others in ways not readily explained by accepted theories.

Similarly, cells in the human embryo know how to cooperatively form the human heart and when to *stop* forming that organ. They are inexplicably connected to one another for the benefit of the whole. Their relational ties defy our understanding.

We, too, are inexplicably connected to a beneficent fabric of relationships. The living fabric of relationships partially reveals itself in *synchronicities*—the meaningful coincidences of life.

Psychologist Carl Jung coined the term "synchronicity" to refer to those coincident outer events and relationships that are packed with significant meaning for an individual's inner development. Synchronicities are sometimes most visible in those unusual personalities whose call becomes manifest in some significant public role of leadership. The biographies of inspirational leaders like Mahatma Gandhi, Eleanor Roosevelt, or Abraham Lincoln can be rich in synchronicities.

Lincoln's path to the White House, for example, seemed synchronously orchestrated. Some of the synchronicities that delivered him there arrived as love relationships.

As a vulnerable young man, Lincoln fell in love with a sensitive young woman, Ann Rutledge. She was the light of his life, as well as a comfort to his introverted soul. She became very sick and died before they could be married. After her death, he fell into deep, nearly catatonic grief. A friend said, "The shadows of a burning he had been through were fixed in the depths of his eyes,"

Yet, she had illuminated a vision of possibilities in him that transcended his limited self-image. He ventured into a political career and set out anew to find a spouse. As an Illinois legislator in Springfield, Illinois, he met, through a friend, Mary Todd; she had come to Springfield hoping to find a husband. Her ambition seemed synchronized with Lincoln's future; she intended to marry a future President of the United States.

From an eager group of attractive and well-heeled suitors, she chose Lincoln—the least likely candidate—against the protests of her family. She must have apprehended in the shy, homely Lincoln a potential for greatness.

Lincoln was stirred by her unlikely affection—so nervously stirred that he could not bring himself to the wedding. He backed out at the last minute without mustering an explanation. He may have intuitively seen that his marriage to Mary would propel him into a career that would consume his life.

He seemed to try, as so many do, to *avoid* the call, fearful of how it might alter the course of his life. Like Jonah who sought to avoid the call to Nineveh, Lincoln found himself in the belly of the whale—the "whale" of depression, confusion, and despair. He wrote during the months of withdrawal that followed, "I am now the most miserable man living. If what I feel were equally distributed to the whole of the human family, there would not be a cheerful face on earth."

When Lincoln found his way back from the depths of despair, he again asked Mary Todd to marry him. Their marriage invigorated that series of events that would eventually propel him to the presidency. By way of various crucial events, this reserved, lanky country lawyer became one of the most admired men in history.

Our own lives may not be as historically momentous, but we too live lives rich in these kinds of meaningful coincidences. We may be seldom conscious of them, but as our attunement to the call grows, so does our awareness of guiding synchronicities.

Be Willing

We are born into this unusual world without much explicit guidance. The great religious traditions of the world do provide important direction, and we will look more closely at that guidance in the next chapter, but we do not get *individual* instructions for our particular lives. There is no owner's manual for our specific life circumstances. At first blush, we seem to have been left adrift to navigate our journeys unaided.

Yet upon closer examination, we learn that we have not been abandoned; we are not without guidance. We are given our *call within* and its many resonant reminders to chart a course to our individual destinies.

Follow your calling, no matter how dimly you may now perceive it. Do something. Act. Find some interest or activity that you can pursue right now, right where you are, and you will begin to move along a seamless web of relationships and events in the direction of your fondest dreams. Serendipitous events and relationships will support you and help to keep you on course.

Whether your calling starts large or small does not matter. Whether you have been sent into this world to cheer and clap for others or to save a democracy, pursue your calling with all your heart.

You may not feel that you are sufficiently equipped for your calling. Do not let that stop you. You will become more fully equipped as you go along. It is far better to aim too high than it is to aim too low, never feeling pressed to develop your full capabilities. A story about a golden eagle illustrates the point.

A young Indian boy, for a prank, removed the egg of a golden eagle from its nest and placed it in the nest of a prairie chicken. The eagle hatched about the same time as the chicks of the prairie chicken. It spent the early months of its life living like a prairie chicken. It learned to scratch like a prairie chicken, cackle like a prairie chicken, and scrounge for food with the rest of the prairie chickens. Then one day the young eagle looked up and saw a beautiful golden eagle soaring in the sky above it.

"What's that?!" exclaimed the young eagle.

"*That* is the golden eagle, the most noble of all birds," said one of the prairie chickens. "But don't give it a thought. *You* could never possibly be like a golden eagle."

The young eagle took the advice of his prairie chicken friend and returned to scratching for food. He grew old and died, never considering that he, too, was a golden eagle.

A small self-concept too often stops us from discovering our true selves. We do not fathom the full resources that we could bring to bear until we take the constraining lid off our tightly compressed self-esteem. It is not a happy feeling to approach the end of life regretting that we did not have the courage to fulfill our own promising potential.

Reach for the most that you can imagine. If you fail, that's okay; failure is part of the process. Failure is success in disguise, for it provides abundant opportunities to successfully *learn* and *adapt*. While the reasons for success may not be clear, the reasons for failure are usually obvious. Fail early and often so that you can succeed sooner!

Feeling that you do not have the necessary resources may also feel limiting; yet, you have access to resources that may go untapped if you underestimate your full potential. Your gifts are drawn from a deep well of resources. The depth of that well cannot be realized until you become committed to a purpose that is greater than your own self-interest. If you feel called to a large undertaking, then large resources begin to appear, either from within you or from others who may feel motivated by your purpose.

Personal history, too, may stop you from pursuing the call within. You can spend much time brooding about what went wrong in the past. That is as disastrous as attempting to drive a car by looking through the rearview mirror. A calling pulls you forward into new, uncharted territory. Leave the past behind if it does not serve you. Allow yourself to become new, to be reborn with a new consciousness of your larger identity and why you are here.

Other people may try to stop you. People who do not have the courage to pursue their call may not want others to pursue theirs either. They may derive comfort in knowing that you, too, have chosen to follow *their* standards. Choices are always easier and less challenging when following the crowd, but the herd does not hold the compass of your individual destiny. The call within is a call to differentiate your life, not to conform to the judgments of others.

Be bold. Find your unique way. You are individually brilliant and noble in some way that your calling will make clear. Find friends who admire and support your unique qualities. Find strength in your growing connection to the germinating call within you, and gain support from others who have also courageously launched their lives in pursuit of that sublime adventure.

What is your calling? What calls you out of the ordinary into the extraordinary? What is that purpose that would require leaving self-absorption behind? Look for it and step forward, willing to let go of your tight control. Being committed to a calling larger than your individual well-being will provide a confident and stabilizing direction. It is a direction that may separate you from the current conforming herd, but that will also align you with the liberating relationships of eternity.

There is a special purpose for your life, if you are willing to heed the call. *Willing* is the key word. You must be willing. You may not feel worthy or fully equipped. Seldom does one feel fully equipped or deserving at the onset. That comes later. More importantly, are you willing?

The quotations following each chapter echo the chapter's themes and affirm a mutual life experience that transcends time, place, and person.

Nobody sees a flower—really—it is so small it takes time—we haven't time—and to see takes time, like to have a friend takes time.

Georgia O'Keefe

Every heart longs to be part of something big and sacred.

Matthew Fox

For what is lost in so many lives, and what must be recovered: a sense of personal calling, that there is a reason I am alive. There is a reason my unique person is here and that there are things I must attend to beyond the daily round and that give the daily round its reason, feelings that the world somehow wants me to be here, that I am answerable to an innate image, which I am filling out in my biography.

James Hillman

This is a call to service that will take great courage— to leave what we have and move out, not without fear, but without succumbing to that fear.

Joseph Jaworski

The free man is he who wills without arbitrary self-will. He believes in destiny, and believes that it stands in need of him . . . He listens to what is emerging from himself, to the source of being in the world; not in order to be supported by it, but in order to bring it to reality as it desires.

Martin Buber

Just as there are no little people or unimportant lives, there is no insignificant work.

Elena Bonner

You are here to enrich the world, and you impoverish yourself if you forget the errand.

Woodrow Wilson

This is the true joy in life, the being used for a purpose recognized by yourself as a mighty one . . . the being a force of nature instead of a feverish, selfish little clod of ailments and grievances complaining that the world will not devote itself to making you happy.

George Bernard Shaw

There is a vitality, a life force, an energy, a quickening, that is translated through you into action, and because there is only one of you in all time, this expression is unique. And if you block it, it will never exist through any other medium and will be lost.

Martha Graham

We don't invent our mission, we detect it. It is within us, waiting to be realized.

Stephen Covey

In work, do what you enjoy.

Lao Tse

Chapter 1: Awakening to the Call

There comes a time in every man's education when he arrives at the conviction that envy is ignorance, that imitation is suicide, that he must take himself for better or worse as his portion; that though the wide universe is full of good, no kernel of nourishing corn can come to him but through the toil bestowed on that plot of ground which is given him to till . . . Trust thyself: every heart vibrates to that iron string.

Ralph Waldo Emerson

Most of us go to our graves with our music still in us.

Oliver Wendell Holmes

The future belongs to those who believe in the beauty of their dreams.

Eleanor Roosevelt

Whether you think you can or think you can't, you're right.

Henry Ford

The outward work can never be small if the inward one is great, and the outward work can never be great or good if the inward one is small or of little worth.

Meister Eckhart

We like to pretend it is hard to follow our heart's dreams. The truth is, it is difficult to avoid walking through the many doors that will open.

Julia Cameron

. . . as if from nowhere, comes the guide: something or someone to help us toward the threshold of adventure. This may take the form of voices within or people who guide us to see the way.

Joseph Jaworski

When a woman falls in love with the magnificent possibilities within herself, the forces that would limit those possibilities hold less and less sway over her.

Marianne Williamson

I had a sense of destiny, as though my life was assigned to me by fate and had to be fulfilled . . . Often I had the feeling that in all decisive matters, I was no longer among men, but was alone with God.

Carl Jung

Everyone should carefully observe which way his heart draws him, and then choose that way with all his strength.

Hasidic saying

If you deliberately plan to be less than you are capable of being, then I warn you, you will be unhappy for the rest of your life. You will be evading your own capabilities, your own possibilities.

Abraham Maslow

We must not allow other people's limited perceptions to define us.

Virginia Satir

Chapter Two

The Way of the Spirit

It gives me a deep comforting sense that "things seen are temporal and things unseen are eternal."

Helen Keller

A calling beckons us to become the unique individuals we were born to become—to differentiate ourselves—and the call is persistent. The full attainment of the call always seems to evade us, although it entices us to press on. Always there, like the whisper of a gentle wind, it urges us forward.

It is the forward movement that matters most—who we are becoming rather than who we have been. We can forget our past mistakes, our limiting biography, and our nattering self-absorption. Just as a rising dawn slowly opens a new day, the calling gradually illuminates a new view of life. The dawning light renders increasingly clear a differentiated destiny, and with it, a more compassionate way of life.

We each have our important individual calling in life—that which inspires us, uses our best gifts, and engages our enthusiasm. In the end, though, what have we really accomplished through our lives in this world? What enduring contribution will we have made?

Whatever our calling, our specific contributions here will most likely be forgotten. In just a few short generations, our lives will have been erased from living memories. Even stories of family members do not usually persist beyond a few generations. Most people know little, if anything, about the grandparents of their grandparents. The arduous and persistent accomplishments of our lives seem to vanish unnoticed into "thin air"; we will not likely leave an enduring contribution in this world.

Even the politically or socially renowned—the people of our day who seem larger than life—will be forgotten. The sonnet "Ozymandias" reminds us of the ultimate earthly insignificance of even the most powerful figures in history. The poet, Percy Shelley, portrays the life of Ramesses the Great, renowned ruler of ancient Egypt. Shelley describes the remains of what was once the colossal statue of Ramesses standing amongst the astonishing engineering accomplishments of his reign. The chiseled inscription on the stone pedestal of this august statue captures the hubris to which those of great accomplishments can be prone:

Look on my works, ye Mighty, and despair!

Shelley tells us that the statue, along with the remnants of that mighty civilization, now consists only of that lone pedestal and a few shattered fragments of the original sculpture:

Nothing beside remains: round the decay
Of that colossal wreck, boundless and bare,
The lone and level sands stretch far away.

Our material accomplishments, no matter how monumental, will also be someday buried by the lone and level sands of relentless time.

This World is Not *It*

Yet, something enduring *is* created by our lives in this world, though it is not *of* this world. We can feel that truth in the very depths of our souls. This world is not *it*—the end-all and be-all purpose for our lives. It is *the means* to an end.

Whether we have been born to lead a country or to shepherd a class of children, a larger and more enduring purpose permeates all that we do. Our work contributes to the growth of something else, something more lasting than the worldly products of our efforts. A momentous, transcendent endeavor is being fashioned amidst the noise and haste of our daily lives.

This world is just a bridge; we cannot expect to build our permanent home upon it. Our real home does not consist of furniture and dust. It lies well beyond the perceptual capacities of this world. Our eternal home is built not on the shifting sands of possessions, position, or prestige, but on the permanent bedrock of *spirit.* Our task is to invest our time and treasure in building a home on *that* solid ground.

The Spirit Guardian

We tend to think of the divine as being unfathomably above and beyond us. Certainly, the Creator and First Cause of our vast universe with its countless galaxies must be far beyond and above our mortal grasp. The Absolute Source and Center of all that is or will ever be is surely incomprehensible to our limited mental frameworks. Yet ancient sages and prophets have also known God to be responsive and close at hand.

They seemed to grasp the presence of the divine more clearly than we empirically grounded moderns do. They were still connected by myth and legend to the instruction of their own ancient ancestors—those prodigious giants of old, known to them as the "sons of God."

We glimpse in the traditions they passed along to us that God is *also* intimately present, self-revealing, responsive, and available. From China to India to Egypt to Greece, many of the wisest sages among those advanced civilizations of ancient times speak of a living relationship with *spirit*.

Socrates, who in his time was reputed to be the wisest of all, acknowledged his debt to his inner spirit. Calling his divine guide by different names—*spirit guardian, daimon, spiritual manifestation, divine sign*—he said it forewarned him of imminent danger and guided him in his inquiries. He and his divine sign seemed to be in almost perpetual converse. Socrates would sometimes pause, still as a stone, to listen attentively to his spirit guardian.

As Plato records the event, Socrates met death unperturbed, for his spirit guardian had assured him that he had nothing to fear and that his life would go on.

> At all previous times my *familiar prophetic power*, my *spiritual manifestation*, frequently opposed me, even in small matters, when I was about to do something wrong, but now that, as you can see for yourselves, I was faced with what one might think, and what is generally thought to be, the worst of evils, my *divine sign* has not opposed me, either when I left home at dawn, or when I came into court, or at any time that I was about to say something during my speech. Yet in other talks it often held me back in the middle of my speaking, but now it has opposed no word or deed of mine. What do I think is the reason for this? I will tell you. What has happened to me may well be a good thing, and those of us who believe death to be an evil are certainly mistaken. I have convincing proof of this, for it is impossible that my *familiar sign* did not oppose me if I was not about to do what was right.

Some of the oldest and most inspired scriptures in the world, the Hindu *Upanishads*, describe the guardian spirit in other terms. In India, the spirit guide was referred to variously as the *Spirit, Self,* or *Atman*.

> For a man who has known [the Self], the light of truth shines; for one who has not known, there is darkness. The wise who have seen him in every being, on leaving this life, attain life immortal.

> What lies beyond life shines not to those who are childish, or careless, or deluded by wealth. 'This is the only world: there is no other,' they say; and thus they go from death to death.

> The Creator made the senses outward-going: they go to the world of matter outside, not to the Spirit within. But a sage who sought immortality looked within himself and found his own Soul.

> When the wise knows that it is through the great and omnipresent Spirit in us that we are

conscious in waking or in dreaming, then he goes beyond sorrow.

When he knows that Atman, the Self, the inner life, who enjoys like a bee the sweetness of the flowers of the senses, the Lord of what was and of what will be, then he goes beyond fear.

The Egyptians—whose towering civilization awed even the prodigious Greeks—knew the inner guide as the *Ka*. Their renowned ancestors had taught that people are given a Ka at birth; it attends them in life and goes with them into the afterlife.

The wisdom of Amenemope, one of Egypt's eminent teachers, found its way into Hebrew Scriptures.

It is the Lord [Ka] who directs a man's steps.
The Lord [Ka] shines into a man's very soul.

Happy is the man who does not take the wicked for his guide, nor walk the road that sinners tread nor take his seat among the scornful; the law of the Lord [Ka] is his delight, the law his meditation night and day. He is like a tree planted beside a watercourse, which yields its fruit in season and its leaf never withers.

Of the mighty prophets who encouraged the Israelites during their Babylonian exile, one called Isaiah unequivocally affirmed that the Lord is intimately and compassionately close at hand.

> Thus says the Lord, the one who created you, who formed you: "Do not be afraid, for I have delivered you. I have called you by name, and you are mine. When you pass through the waters, I will be with you; and through the rivers, they shall not overcome you. When you walk through the fire, you shall not be burned, and the flame shall not consume you . . . You are precious in my sight, and I love you . . . Do not be afraid— for I am with you."

Referred to by different names in different cultures, the spirit guardian has served to stabilize and direct the lives of individuals, and with them whole civilizations, for millennia. In our modern "enlightened" age—saturated in materialism, lulled by the promises of empirical science, jarred by the paroxysms of change—we are too often prone to ignore the sacred living experience with the spirit guardian.

The largely unconscious spirit might be thought of like a keel to a sailboat. The keel is the slim extension at the bottom of the hull that forms the "backbone" of the sailboat. It keeps the boat from skimming wildly over the surface. It is under the boat, unseen, and always in the water. The keel stabilizes the sails that catch the wind and power the craft. The sails are visible, lofty, and prestigious; but the keel is deep in the water, always at work, quietly and invisibly providing stability.

Like the keel of a sailboat, the spirit holds our lives fast in the psychic water of our souls. The spirit stabilizes the ship of conscious life. It influences all that we do. Without the sails of our ego, there would be no assertive movement through conscious life, but without the keel, the first troublesome gust of wind would send our ship of consciousness careening out of control.

The spirit is *with* us, but not *us*, not even of this world. It calls to us, and much of life is unknowingly lived in response to the minute-to-minute influence of spirit. Our common consummate purpose in life is to respond to spirit, to yield and dedicate our lives to the outworking of its inner call. It is our common work of everlasting import. Beside that great work, everything else is trivial.

We grow to completion and wholeness by joining our lives to the spirit within us. Until we commit to the spirit's deeper call, our lives feel superficially disjoined. Life seems like a doubly exposed photograph—two images seeking expression in one frame.

Our relationship to the spirit guardian is never dull or stagnant; it fills every cubit and cranny of our waking or dormant lives. The spirit relentlessly encourages our growth to wholeness. We may feel depressed, resistant, disturbed, confused, or wistful; yet, these moments of confusion, pause, or depression often precede stretches of clarity and optimism.

When one coveted door closes, another unexpected door often opens, ushering in new and larger possibilities. Abandoning a way of life, acknowledging an error, delighting in a new pursuit, leaving some comfortable habit behind—these can all be expressions of our intimate relationship with spirit.

We may often feel impelled to restructure our lives to allow a more fulfilling way of life to emerge. The way of the spirit is the way of eternal import; it renders an otherwise fleeting life with extraordinary eternal significance.

The Way

If we knew more about the way of the spirit guide, we might be better equipped to live as fully committed partners. We are so often unconscious of the holiness of everyday activity. We too often dismiss day-to-day ideas, conversations, thoughts, preoccupations, and passions as *ordinary*. We treat it all as common.

Though our awareness of the spirit may be faint, others have been acutely awake to the brilliance of that inner light. They have, in turn, illuminated a path serviceable for us all.

Much that we know about the *way* of the spirit comes from those who have been unusually moved by it—the mystics, prophets, sages, and philosophers through the ages. One century in particular, the sixth century BC, was fertile with an uncanny conjunction of enlightened individuals around the world. They gave birth to a renaissance that would illumine the lives of people for centuries. What they taught and established over twenty-five hundred years ago remains entrenched in the cultures of the world today.

In Greece, the seeds of today's democracies were sown, science and mathematics were established, and philosophy was born. In China, Lao Tse and Confucius built traditions that would hold the social fabric of that country together for over twenty-five hundred years. In Northern India, Guatama Siddhartha established the precepts of Buddhism. In the Middle East, the Hebrew people, threatened with extinction, tenaciously cohered and the book we know as the Bible took form.

From Greece to Persia to India to China, the world's major civilizations experienced a profound religious and intellectual renaissance. Discerning sages taught people about "the way." The very word *Tao*, from Lao Tse's Taoism, means *The Way*. Confucius frequently spoke of "The Way of Heaven." For Buddha, it was the "Eightfold Path" and the "Middle Way." The prophets admonished the Hebrew people to follow "The Way of the Lord." Each was a way of compassion and humility.

Lao Tse spoke of the Tao—the way of the universe, the way of ultimate reality. Find the Tao, he taught, and center your life there. Out of that connection comes a life of virtue, a *creative quietude*, a freedom and access to abundant resources when the self-important ego yields to the presence of the Tao.

Similarly, the Greek philosopher Heraclitus recognized the *Logos*—the Greek equivalent of the Tao. Both terms acknowledge the unseen living architecture of the divine, present everywhere and throughout all time. Discover the way of the *Logos*, for it is the way of life eternally.

The idea of the *Logos* seemed to float through the centuries like a feather descending to earth, finding a receptive breeze in the emerging Stoic philosophy of Greece. It wafted into Hebrew theology through Philo of Alexandria, ultimately coming to rest in John's Gospel of the Christian New Testament, parsimoniously translated today as the "Word" of God.

Confucius advocated a life of virtue and carefully prescribed how that life would be lived. He coined the *silver rule*: "What you do not wish done to yourself, do not do to others." He advocated a life of duty, balance, honor, and goodness as "The Way of Heaven."

Buddha, "The Awakened One," established a way "of infinite compassion." Like Socrates in Greece, he advocated returning good for evil. He taught, "Overcome anger by love, overcome evil by good," and "Consider others as yourself." Speaking of the interminable struggle with selfish desire, he said, "He is greater who conquers himself than he who conquers a whole army."

Together, these and other "awakened" teachers of the sixth century BC, established many of the tenets, mores, philosophies, and traditions that shaped the enduring foundation of civilization—for both East and West.

The Eternal Gospel

Nearly six hundred years later, a carpenter's son in Galilee artfully wove the threads of East and West into the gracious tapestry that he called the "gospel of the kingdom of heaven." Like his Eastern predecessors, he advocated a way of self-forgetful compassion. Like Isaiah of the Babylonian captivity and Socrates in the Golden Age of Greece, he spoke of an attentive, compassionate God.

Jesus of Nazareth traveled the countryside with his twelve apostles and seventy trained evangelists conveying a simple and profoundly important "gospel":

God loves each of us intimately.

The way that he advocated is the way of simple compassion:

Love one another.

His gospel is alive and available in the stories he used to illustrate his teaching. His parables portray a compassionate God who is eager to welcome us, constantly searching for us within our own inner lives.

Jesus taught that God is attentive even to the seemingly minor events of life, even when a sparrow falls from a tree. He spoke of the hairs of our heads being "numbered" to portray how intimately acquainted God is with our individual lives.

He portrayed God as the merchant in search of a pearl of great value. We are that pearl.

He spoke figuratively of God as the attentive shepherd willing to go in search of even just one lost lamb. We are that lamb.

He used the image of a woman sweeping in relentless pursuit of a coin. We are that coin that the relentless God searches for amidst the dusty cares of daily life.

In the touching portrayal of the prodigal son who leaves his home and squanders his life, Jesus taught that God is ever ready to welcome us home with open arms, without regard to how we may have spent our lives.

Jesus often spoke metaphorically about a "kingdom of heaven." His words about the kingdom seem, on the surface, incongruous. To one he said, "The kingdom of heaven is not of this world," yet to another he said, "You are not far from the kingdom."

It is close at hand yet not *of* this world. How can we make sense of this apparent contradiction? He also taught, "The kingdom of heaven is within you." This statement solves the conundrum. This figurative kingdom could be near at hand yet not of this world, *if* it is the spiritual presence of God within our souls. He explicitly taught that, to enter this kingdom, one must be "born of the spirit."

He likened the kingdom to a mustard seed, which starts small yet grows to immense proportions. He said the kingdom is like leaven to bread—that which initiates growth. These metaphors speak of the spiritual presence of God, actively engaged as a catalyst, growing the infrastructure of our enduring lives.

His story of a man finding a treasure in a field illustrated the value of the inner spirit. When the man in the parable found the treasure, he was willing to give up all that he had to own the field and the treasure within it. Such is the value of *our* spiritual treasure in the field of the soul.

On another occasion he taught that we do not enter this kingdom unless we become as small children. Jesus lived a life of implicit trust in the attentive guidance of the one he called "Abba" (Papa), trusting God as a small child trusts a parent. "Seek first the kingdom of heaven, and its righteousness," he taught, "and all things needful will be provided." "Be not concerned about tomorrow, enough are the troubles of today."

Entering the kingdom is not dependent on following preset codes of conduct. Rather, Jesus encouraged people to respond creatively to life, freely drawing on the intimate inspiration and guidance of the spirit.

Jesus exhorted his followers to forgive always, to suspend judgment, to love even enemies, to return good for evil, and to serve everyone—even the "least among you." He taught that if someone demands that we carry a pack for a mile, we should carry it not only the first mile, but also a second to show our good will.

Jesus lived what he taught. He was forever attentive to his own spirit guide; he lived a life wholly dedicated to that invaluable living relationship. The way of Jesus, born from this transcendent spiritual "kingdom," was simple: Love God and love others.

The Rewards of the Way

Few people over the last two thousand years have had the courage to exercise Jesus' positive love. For us to make the effort to live such a devoted life, there must be a *reward*. There must be a prize that draws us out of the easier life of self-centeredness.

Our relationship with the spirit *is* that prize. As we give up self-absorption, we draw closer to what is real and enduring. When we love with his degree of second-mile compassion, we establish a living connection to the spirit within. That connection is worth any price to attain, for the rewards of life with the spirit are priceless.

We experience the peace and happiness that "passes all understanding"; we discover the Tao, the Logos of life, and the creative quietude that accompanies it.

In that living connection, we are liberated from anxiety. We may not know what the future holds, but we know that a compassionate and attentive God holds our future. We are assured that the curtain of death will not bring an end to our lives; rather, it will be the opening curtain to the next enthralling theater.

We are freed from the constraints of conformity, liberated to develop as unique individuals, less encumbered with traditional conventions or superficial concerns about position or standing.

We are born to a secure and enduring relationship. The spirit is our constant companion—always alert, ever available, and tirelessly responding in every minute of our lives.

The spirit frees us from the isolating restraints of selfishness. Intolerance, prejudice, envy, arrogance, greed, blame, equivocation, self-righteousness, slothfulness, or pride—these are all forms of selfishness. When we are in the grip of these natural human tendencies, we may think that we are "right." In learning to be *kind*, rather than *right*, we gain relationships with others—the heart of happiness.

These are the abundant rewards of the way of the spirit. If you want to experience these rewards, start by going the extra mile. Extend a simple kindness, forgive a hurt, mend a quarrel, or give a soft answer. Seize the courage to live that way, and *then* decide whether the way of the spirit is worth the price. You be the judge, based on your own personal experience.

You can trust the presence of the spirit within to lead you—to effectively and persistently keep your call before you. It calls you to more than just doing a certain type of work; it calls you to venture beyond conventional thinking and to transcend selfishness.

You may be required to release various forms of selfishness. You may have to give up self-limiting thoughts about past mistakes, inadequacies, or misfortunes. You may have to give up self-righteousness or arrogance. You may be required to be born anew.

Sages and prophets from Buddha to Jesus have illuminated the way of the spirit. It is a way in which you are freed from what may repress you, freed to find and follow an inner calling, and freed to love generously.

I have called this center the self . . . it might equally be called the "God within us." The beginnings of our whole psychic life seem to be inextricably rooted in this point, and all our highest and ultimate purposes seem to be striving towards it.

Carl G. Jung

God is at home; it is we who have gone out for a walk.

Meister Eckhart

When your life is filled with the desire to see the holiness in everyday life, something magical happens: Ordinary life becomes extraordinary, and the very process of life begins to nourish your soul.

Harold Kushner

There has been an unseen River of God which, like the rivers beneath the city of Damascus, has flowed on with quickening waters of Life underneath the onward course of History . . .

Rufus Jones

Overcome anger by love, overcome evil by good. Overcome the miser by giving, overcome the liar by truth.

Buddha

Do not worry if people do not recognize your merits; worry that you may not recognize theirs.

Confucius

Do not look at the faults of others, or what others have done or not done; observe what you yourself have done and have not done.

Buddha

Why do you look at the speck of sawdust in your brother's eye, with never a thought for the great plank in your own?

Jesus

The first peace, which is most important, is that which comes within the souls of people when they realize their relationship, their oneness, with the universe and all its powers, and when they realize that at the center of the universe dwells the Great Spirit, and that this center is really everywhere, it is within each of us.

Black Elk

Love your enemies, do good to those who hate you, bless those who curse you, pray for those who abuse you. From anyone who takes away your coat do not withhold even your shirt.

Jesus

I don't know what your destiny will be, but one thing I know: The only ones among you who will really be happy are those who have sought and found how to serve.

Albert Schweitzer

It is within my power either to serve God or not to serve him. Serving him, I add to my own good and the good of the whole world. Not serving him, I forfeit my own good and deprive the world of that good, which was in my power to create.

Leo Tolstoy

For this purpose we have been created: to love and to be loved.

Mother Teresa

Chapter Three

The Journey of Discovery

Whatever you can do, or dream you can, begin it. Boldness has genius, power and magic in it.

Goethe

It is fine to *talk* about following a calling; it is noble to think about living a compassionate life, but we must *do* these things. What good is the thought if it has no complement in action—in becoming tangibly real in day-to-day life? If any of this is to become valuable, it must be *acted* upon.

Once fully committed to your own call within, the burden may often seem easy and the "yoke" light. You will probably get much unexpected help.

Yet, it may also be true that you must cross a desert of uncertainty to discover the refreshing oasis of your call. In ushering a vague and barely discernible call into your conscious life, there will likely be a struggle—the struggle for your renewed life.

You may be required to do a great deal of work or study. Doors might seem to close in your face. You could experience despair and almost unbearable frustration. Trusted friends might betray you. Your life may seem destined for failure and ruin. You may feel lodged in the shoals of misfortune. You might feel that the entire universe has turned against you. You could come to despise the call and all that seems to accompany it. You may question the compassion of God and wonder if life is really worth living.

These are the moments to savor.

When things seem the darkest, when every step we take seems to be into a dismal ditch, the time is ripe for the next quantum leap, the next epiphany. These are the bleak but happy times that affirm our commitment and strengthen our characters. Outwardly they may seem discouraging, but inwardly we instinctively know that our resolve is being fashioned hard as steel. These are the times that open a new door, deliver a lesson, prune the moral branches, or fertilize the psychic soil.

When you find your world crumbling and collapsing around you, take heart. These are the signs that the spirit is active in your life. You are on the threshold of something grander, more vital, and more authentic. You are moving as though through a dense and entangling forest into an open clearing. Your life is being reborn into something more purposeful than you previously knew.

These are the times when we learn to trust that the spirit is at work for us, that our course feels charted, as the planets in their orbits are charted through space and time. Even though life may be showing up as chaos, despair, or frustration, we can learn to trust that the spirit has hold of our lives and that we will emerge more whole, complete, and authentic than before the struggle.

Deny the struggle, attempt to circumvent that which the spirit has called you forth to endure, and you will never know your own strength, your own capabilities, or the possibility of the unlived life waiting within you.

Strong characters are forged on the anvils of time by the hammers of difficulty. To forge a strong character, the hammer is sometimes necessary. As Tennyson understood, life is not as idle ore . . .

> But iron, dug from central gloom,
> And heated hot with burning fears,
> And dipt in baths of hissing tears,
> And Batter'd with the shocks of doom
>
> To shape and use.

Struggling to attain the call has intrinsic value. It is an opportunity to experience the road of trials. We develop stronger wills. We learn that ego-gratification alone is not sufficiently satisfying—that there is no gold at the end of that rainbow.

We are like a butterfly struggling to emerge from the chrysalis. The butterfly strengthens its wings by struggling its way out. If prematurely released from its chrysalis, it will languish hopelessly on the ground, lacking the strength to spread its wings and fly. If the butterfly does not take on the *fight*, it is incapable of *flight*.

Struggles also strengthen us for a new life. Like the butterfly, we too are liberated from a heavy, lumbering, earth-bound way of life into a renewed, lighter, more uplifting one.

We are not coerced into that transformation; we can choose to stay in the dark chrysalis of our comfortable lives. The spirit encourages, cajoles, entangles, frustrates, but never seems to *force* us to heed the call. That choice is ours.

The Monastery of the World

We are not just called to do some specific work, to follow our interests, or to use our gifts. It is bigger than that. We are called to become unique individuals with strong characters. That call manifests in all that we do—what we read, whom we befriend, how we relate to others, the relationships we cultivate, the struggles we endure, the conflicts we resolve, our willingness to forgive, our efforts to understand. It appears in the fullness of our commitment to bring all of our resources to life. The spirit calls us forward to completion, to the fulfillment of our potential. It is for us to follow that deep and pressing call to grow toward the center and circumference of our destiny.

When we live life this way, finding our call from minute to minute, we find the spirit in the streets and in the nooks and crannies of everyday life. The world—the place where our gifts are offered, where our forgiveness and our service are given, where our struggles and failures are endured—becomes our monastery. This is where we find the living spirit—here within us and around us, in the midst of our day-to-day experience.

It is in this monastery of the world that we also find ourselves. Here we gradually lose our pretentious facades. These social personas serve a useful function as insulating barriers; they protect our vulnerability, but in following the call, the artificiality of those personas is eroded. We become more deeply rooted and integrated with what is real and true. All that is false about us begins to fall away like disintegrating rusted armor.

In the monastery of the world, we find the human relationships that renew us. Attention to the well-being of others keeps us on that precious path that delivers the supreme joy of life. It is not as much what we *get* from these relationships, but what we *give*, that is important. To grow more vital in life, we give ourselves away daily. Though outwardly we grow older, inwardly, in the *sanctum sanctorum* of the soul, we become *newer.*

The spirit calls us to differentiate ourselves, to fulfill the destiny that is embedded in our hearts and that destiny is never completely fulfilled. Each plateau of character development reached on the journey up the mountain of our call reveals the more enthralling, more compelling path to the next plateau. We learn along the way that it is not the destination that thrills us as much as the journey. We fall in love with the journey of growth, for as Cervantes observed, "The journey is better than the inn."

In that journey, you may arrive at a time when you begin to throw out unwanted baggage, for it can slow you down. You do not want more stuff in your life; you want less—less of the luggage of conformity or the trappings of material one-upmanship. You only want what is necessary for the journey.

So you may bail, unloading persistently and methodically in hopes of getting to the heart of your passion. You may be compelled, as St. Francis and Mother Teresa were compelled, to keep your daily life and your belongings simple so that you may be freed to keep your inner life abundant and alive.

Keeping the inner life abundant and alive also has its consequences in the outer life. Not only do we unload unwanted baggage, we also engage more fully in our work and our relationships. Our life in the outer world increasingly becomes an expression of our inner life. The two seem to merge—charmed forth by synchronicity.

We make a decision to act, perhaps after much brooding or contemplation, and that one simple decision to act is a catalyst for other events. Resources and assistance appear from unexpected sources. The very act of living boldly, as Goethe noted, has magical and powerful consequences. We meet the people, encounter the circumstances, read the article or the book that confirm our decisions and assist us along our way. The outer world becomes an expression and a confirmation of the inner passion.

The reverse also occurs. What we make real in the conscious life has its complement in the inner life, engendering thoughts, images, dreams, inspirations, or ideas. When the inner life and outer life are reinforcing one another, we feel that life is "flowing"; our work and our relationships seem almost effortless. Life is good.

But there are also the *other* times, the times when there is no flow. The flow has become a "clunk," like jammed machinery. Some recurring issue or event may have stopped us short; an old, nagging problem may have reappeared. We may feel off-balance, out of focus, or depressed. We may feel bored or distant, or we may be besieged by quarrels and confrontation; no one seems to be living up to our expectations of them, nor are we living up to our own.

These are the times that are fertile with opportunity. These are the times to question, *What is amiss? What needs adjusting?* When we are in the throes of an emotional whirlwind, it is hard to see our lives objectively. We need to transcend the turmoil and become observers rather than reactive victims. We may need to pause to get a fresh perspective.

At those times, it is often helpful to find something that relaxes and refreshes our minds: reading a good book, watching a lighthearted film, taking a walk in a natural setting, listening to restful music, talking with a friend. Sometimes that is all we need, for with rest some problems take flight on their own.

But if they persist, then it can be helpful to ask certain *catalytic questions*.

Catalytic Questions

Asking the right questions can deliver a treasure of insight and wisdom. When your life seems derailed by a perplexing dilemma, responding to evocative questions can deliver greater perspective, stamina, and insight. Use those times when you feel stuck or jammed to discover some new understanding, for, as Joseph Campbell noted, "Where you stumble, there your treasure is."

Any of the following eight catalytic questions can help to unlock that treasure. At those times when you feel derailed, choose one or more of these questions to help you get back on track. Start with the question that seems to have the most energy—the one that feels like it holds the greatest potential for addressing your dilemma.

Any one of these questions can be like a grain of sand to an oyster: It may feel a little uncomfortable at first, but can also produce the pearl of a purposeful life.

1. How am I gifted?

Your natural gifts—your aptitudes—are like a compass heading for the call. They point the way, offering assurance that you are on the right course. Work that uses your best gifts is more effortlessly enjoyable, more satisfying, and often more materially rewarding.

Gifts are certainly not the only component of a calling. A calling may not even pertain to the work you do, *necessarily*; it may have more to do with the attitude and character you bring to *any* work. Still, any work is easier if it uses your best gifts.

How do you know which are your best gifts? The answer to that question is so obvious that many people miss it: Look at what you naturally *enjoy doing*. It is as obvious as water to a fish. Yet, just as a fish may not be conscious of the water that sustains it, you may not be fully aware of the gifts that have sustained you all your life.

There is a very simple way to get a sense of direction from your best gifts. When you have about an hour of quiet, dedicated time, complete the following exercise. It will provide a "compass heading" that orients you to your most enjoyable work.

Make a list of some of the experiences you have most enjoyed. Spend some reflective, uninterrupted time reviewing those experiences that have been effortlessly enjoyable and fulfilling. Draw from all aspects of your life, no matter how far back, recalling any activity or event that you found readily enjoyable or fulfilling.

Write down everything that comes to mind. Quantity is more important than quality. Enjoy the cruise back across your ocean of memories. Remember the positive experiences. Refrain from focusing on any unhappy memories. Don't worry about your spelling, grammar, or form. No one will be reading your list but you. You may have had many experiences or accomplishments that seem insignificant. Record those experiences as well for they will tend to evoke the memories of other, more significant ones.

After completing your list, identify three experiences that seem to stand out, that have the greatest "energy" about them, or that seem to "jump off the page."

Write a brief summary of each, describing only what you enjoyed doing in that experience. What you enjoyed doing could include any aspect of your experience: the physical, relational, productive, contemplative, prophetic, or creative elements.

You need not describe the experiences fully. You are looking only for those aspects of the experience that were especially enjoyable. Ignore any parts that were not enjoyable.

When you finish summarizing your three experiences, look at the following groups of gifts. Each group has a designated "compass heading." Put a check next to the group that is most consistent with what you enjoyed, for each experience. After you review all three of your favored experiences, a preference for one or two of the compass headings should begin to become evident.

Reflective Gifts (NW)

Enjoyed feeling deeply inspired, creative, and moved by inner images. Gained energy and enthusiasm from seeing aesthetic or prophetic possibilities from the inner life where ideas, ideals, and imagination readily flowed.

Associating Gifts (SW)

Enjoyed attending to the physical well-being of others and empathizing with their feelings and values. Gained energy and enthusiasm from relating to others, sharing opinions and feelings, and building harmony among people.

Productive Gifts (SE)

Enjoyed the concrete, practical aspects of life and being productive, oriented to goals, and well organized. Gained energy and enthusiasm from constructing, building, organizing, producing, scheduling, and achieving tangible results.

Formulating Gifts (NE)

Enjoyed contemplating ideas, insights, principles, theories, and abstract concepts. Gained energy and enthusiasm from formulating solutions, especially for complex problems.

(To learn more about each of these four compass headings, visit GiftsCompass.com. You can
also take a self-assessment there that will help
to clarify your preferred gifts.)

Whenever you are considering new work, you
can check in with the results of this exercise to see if
your favored gifts would be used in the work. In this
way, you can look before you leap, learning *in ad-
vance* whether the work uses your best gifts. It is too
easy to plunge into new work that seems exciting,
only to feel stuck and frustrated once fully committed.

If, however, you have already leapt and now
feel stuck, evaluate the work you are doing to see if
you can make adjustments to more fully use your best
gifts. Modifying your current work is often easier
than searching for new work elsewhere.

Referring to your preferred compass heading is
a very helpful means of staying on course with your
best gifts, yet it need not displace a strong sense of
inner guidance. Sometimes your inner spiritual guidance may override logical choices. If you feel a
strong call to undertake something that seems incon-
sistent with your best gifts, you may need to simply
heed that call. The spirit seems to seek "wholeness,"
to bring forth new strengths and to press our full po-

tential. Especially in the second half of life, we often need to develop new, unexplored dimensions of our full capabilities.

2. What does my life "want" to be?

One of the great architects of the twentieth century, Louis Kahn, was an architect of seemingly average ability until he reached his mid-fifties. Then he began to produce some extraordinary architectural designs, almost ethereal in their simplicity. He made it a practice, after thoroughly understanding the programmatic needs for a building, to ask what seemed to be a ridiculous question: "What does the building *want* to be?"

You may think that an inanimate building, which had not yet been designed, did not *want* to be anything. Yet, out of asking that one penetrating question, Kahn received his inspirational images.

Using his approach, you could ask similar questions regarding your life. Listening to the call within is seldom a literal experience of being spoken to with specific words; rather, it can be more like following a vague feeling. Though we may not be able to translate that feeling literally, we can talk about it metaphorically in terms of what it is *like*.

To get the process started, begin with the following few questions that will help to evoke some metaphorical images.

If my life could be like any other person's, either historical or contemporary, whose life would it be like?

If my life could be like any movie or film genre, what movie or film type would it be like?

If my life could be like anything in nature, what would it be like?

After each of your answers, briefly list a few adjectives or descriptive phrases that express what is behind your answer. For example, if in response to the third question you said, "a large oak tree," you might include the following terms to more fully portray your response: stable, reliable, graceful, offering protection to others.

Then finally, ask yourself this open question:

What does my life want to be?

Try to simply remain open to whatever images come in response to this question. There is no need to force them. This is not brainstorming.

Just observe what comes to mind. Find the images that have the greatest sense of import and then describe more fully what that image means for you.

These metaphors, like your gifts, can guide your direction. The metaphors are a way of bringing forth from your soul the dream of a well-lived life. Consider making some adjustments in the way you are living to more fully express these metaphorical images—what your soul "wants to be." Begin looking at those potential changes—subtle or dramatic—that could help your conscious, everyday life become more aligned with these guiding metaphorical images.

3. What if I lived more deliberately?

Henry David Thoreau said he made his reclusive journey into the woods to "live deliberately," so that he would not find, at the end of his life, that he had never truly lived at all. We don't necessarily need to make that physical pilgrimage to live more deliberately; asking the sorts of questions that Thoreau may have asked can produce similar results.

Refreshingly new vistas of purposeful living can be tapped just by asking questions beginning with the words, "What if . . ." The questions, if responded to without a lot of censoring self-talk, can open up a whole new world of possibilities.

When you answer the following "What if . . ." questions, let the critical and judging side of your thinking take a rest; let your imagination roam free. Negative, excessively practical, or judgmental thinking can kill a creative idea before it has time to germinate. Your own pre-judgments can keep you imprisoned in a limiting self-concept and prevent you from freely journeying into your purposeful woods, as Thoreau did.

Spend some time alone somewhere where you can mentally go into your own "woods" and write your response to the following questions:

What if you could do anything with your life that you chose? There are no obstacles to successfully accomplishing anything. Money is not a problem; you have all the money you need to accomplish anything you want to do. Time is not an issue; you have all the time in the world. Talent is not a problem; you are fully capable of accomplishing anything you set out to do.

If you had all that and also knew that you would not fail, what would you do with your life?

What if you were to be transported to the end of your life and you were looking back in a life review?

What would make you feel good about the life you led?

Briefly describe the life that would have been a full and rich life, one for which you would have few regrets.

In taking this sort of imaginative journey, we can get in touch with what is most meaningful, thrilling, and important in our lives. Once we have a clearer vision of where we want to go, we can begin, as Thoreau did, to live more deliberately in the direction of our vision.

Sometimes the most difficult step in a journey is the first one. When you do something, no matter how small, to take your life more deliberately in a direction, the step tends to create momentum and enthusiasm. Then, doing more to keep moving in that direction tends to get easier, for the restraining inertia of inaction has been broken.

4. What anxiety is keeping me from a full and abundant life?

Worry and regret can slow us down or stop us cold. Exaggerated worry taints our anticipation of the future; exaggerated regret sours our memory of the past.

There is a *moderate* role for both. Worry—concern about the future—can help us to circumvent problems before they occur. Regret—misgivings about the past—can help to guide our current decisions so that we do not repeat past mistakes. Obsessing about either will keep us bound up in a straitjacket of self-absorption. They paralyze our ability to live life fully.

When you find yourself shackled by worry or regret, consider the following two approaches:

For Worry

Identify the source of your worry. If it is nothing you can do anything about, then assume that you can trust your future to the attentive spirit. Take that leap of faith. Live as though everything is well in hand, and trust that what you are worrying about will be resolved in due time. Postpone any further worry for thirty days. Then renew that commitment every thirty days until the source of worry has been resolved—one way or the other. Most of the things we worry about never arrive in the dire form we imagined, if they arrive at all.

If there is something you can do about the object of your worry, consider the worst-case scenario. How bad could it all get? Write that out so that it is clear to you. If you are sufficiently disturbed by what you write, identify what you could do to circumvent the dire outcome. Take action if a course of action is available to you and you feel strongly that the object of your worry will happen.

For Regret

Identify what, from your past, is holding you back now. Consider that your regret is there for a reason. There may be a nagging lesson in the memory.

Talk with a friend about it or write out what you think you need to know about that regret. What mistakes did you make? What lesson is there to be learned about the experience? How would you do things differently the next time?

Then write out what you are currently thankful for. That is, count your blessings. Sometimes the things you are currently thankful for would not have been possible without the regretful experiences of the past.

Too often, when we obsess about regrets, they get amplified out of proportion. Talking about them with a friend, understanding their value, or seeing them in the context of all that we may be thankful for can shrink them back to a more manageable size. They may not go away entirely, but they can get small enough, as a mental image, to stop holding us back.

5. What implicit rule binds me to the problem?

Heraclitus, the pre-Socratic Greek philosopher, used to say, "The way down is also the way up." That may not sound very profound. Most of us are already aware of that and don't need a philosopher's help on that point. Yet, when solving problems, we may act as though we *do not* know that to be true.

Sometimes, our way up and out of a problem is by way of the same implicit rule that initially took us down into the problem. Our underlying assumptions themselves keep us unnecessarily restrained.

Picasso once said that the act of creation is first an act of destruction. If we are to create a new life in following the call, our inhibiting assumptions may have to be destroyed.

We carry many of these assumptions (implicit rules) with us virtually unconsciously: "That is never done that way," or "I am too young," or "I am too old," or "You can't do that without an advanced degree," or "That takes too much money," or "*They* would not approve."

These are among several assumed rules, any one of which may have to be broken if we are to find our way up and out of a dilemma that is holding us down.

For any nagging problem that seems to keep holding you back, ask this question:

What are the assumptions or unconscious rules that have me tied up in this problem?

Write down everything you notice. The BIG implicit rule will sometimes figuratively jump off the page—the one that, if it were broken, would really free you up.

Then consider the costs of your being restrained by it: What has that rule stopped you from doing? What have you lost? What will it bar you from in the future?

When we more fully see how a constraining assumption could be holding us back from a more abundant life, we get the impetus to overcome it.

Helen Keller was deaf and blind. One would think that those two considerable impediments would have prevented her from making *any* contribution in life, but they did not.

6. *What would the spirit say?*

As our beneficial relationship with the spirit grows, we discover an elemental principle of the spiritual economy: *Those who have attained much will be given more.*

How then shall we attain more?

There are many ways to build a relationship with the spirit. The longstanding religious traditions and practices provide abundant means. We may also seek a connection through music, art, philosophy, nature, dance, or literature. All of these avenues can bear many fruitful connections.

Prayerful dialogue is also helpful. Prayer need not be a one-sided request or monologue; prayer can also be a *dialogue*. We can talk over the issues of life with our spirit guardian—we can speak *and* listen.

Try the following sometime when you are alone:

Write down whatever is on your mind, writing as though you are talking to a close friend. Listen for a response and write what you feel or imagine the response to be. Continue to write and listen this way until you feel that you have talked an issue through or arrived at some resolution. Writing the imagined dialogue down helps to make the conversation more tangible while it may also help to clarify your life direction.

One of my first such prayerful dialogues was in the Rocky Mountains. I had awakened very early one morning with an urge to walk up the side of a nearby mountain. As I walked, I began to talk and ask questions. To my surprise, silent images of answers faintly arrived. Some of the answers I received on that early walk have guided my life ever since.

It is true that following a sense of calling within can be exhilarating. It is also true that following it can be difficult, confusing, scary, and upsetting. There will be times when we just need to reconfirm our bearings or to get the earth back beneath our feet. Answering any of these six questions at times when we feel indecisive, confused, scared, or angry can help to dissolve the sense of inner chaos that seems inevitable whenever we venture beyond the seemingly safe and secure picket fence of our customary lives.

Follow Your Joy

"Joy," the insightful theologian Pierre Teilhard de Chardin reportedly said, "is the infallible sign of the presence of God." Mindful attention to all that brings joy leads us along the path of a purposeful life. When we follow our joy, we are continually born anew, each day becoming more whole and more *real*.

Too many people have stopped pursuing the joy of a purposeful life, instead settling for the common life that Thoreau called "quiet desperation"—accommodating the social artifice of life in the world rather than the joy that issues from the spiritual life within.

Each night the stars emerge to remind us that we are the fortunate citizens of a vast and generous universe; yet each day we awaken to what may feel like a petty or pernicious world. We seem at times in the middle of the prophetic poem by William Butler Yeats, "The Second Coming": *Things fall apart; the centre cannot hold; Mere anarchy is loosed upon the world.*

The nation states in which we live will someday be thorny bywords in the lexicon of more enlightened people. If we are to find our "centre," individually and as a people, we must draw on the life-giving joy of the soul—the very breath of spirit.

We breathe air that sustains our bodies. Breathing delivers needed oxygen to billions of symbiotic cells. We breathe and we live; should we stop breathing, we would stop living.

Similarly, the spirit's breath of joy sustains our will to live and to live purposefully. We breathe and we love; should we stop breathing the spirit's joy, we would stop loving.

In breathing the spirit's joy, we discover and animate the purposeful life that beckons us. We sustain and grow our enduring lives with that breath.

God is not far off and aloof but present as spirit to our every decision and concern. Though separated in time from other galaxies by sometimes millions of light years, we are not separated from the presence of God by one nanosecond. Alone? No. Isolated? Not for a minute.

We are each beneficently connected to the majestic fabric of cosmic purpose, and without each of us individually, that fabric is diminished, much as the loss of a child in a family leaves an irreplaceable void.

Every atom of every molecule declares that life is connected, that there is a way and a purpose for life. Reductive cosmologists may theorize that the universe was born with a bang and will likely end with a thud. Yet, amidst the dim haze of that narrowly circumscribed view, one immutable fact remains clear and true: the God who knows the number of hairs on our heads, who hangs the earth upon nothing, who upholds the orbits of both electrons and planets, who sustains the living intelligence of life, who compassionately and tirelessly calls each of us to life, will not mindlessly bring the universe to a crushing and inglorious end.

The cosmos may be *respiring*, but it is not *expiring*. There is a grand purpose to the march of the universe through space and time; all of our mortal struggling is not in vain. We are each called to bring a unique and compelling contribution to life.

The spirit that calls us forth is available at every moment of our conscious and our unconscious lives. We meet "the living God" in our call. All of our cosmological hypothesizing and all of our theological dogma will not render our Creator more real than the minute-to-minute experience of attending to the spirit's call within.

Our relationship with the spirit is more real than all the belief systems stacked end to end. The firsthand relationship with spirit is where we not only experience what is real, but also grow more real ourselves.

"What is real?" asked the Velveteen Rabbit in the story by the same name. "Real is what you become," was the uncanny response. "Once you are real, you cannot become unreal again. It lasts for always."

Children's stories, like this one, sometimes contain more value than the more complicated adult social constructs that we too often mistake for reality. Being open to these simple truths and experiences of life may, in part, have been what Jesus meant when he said that to enter the kingdom of heaven, we must become like small children.

Real is something we become as we follow the call in the day-to-day monastery of the world. We do not become more *physically* real; our mortal forms will someday perish. We become more *personally* real. Once we are real, we cannot become unreal again.

Our call within is a summons not just to do a certain work, but also to grow into the full and uniquely valuable *persons* we were born to become. The spirit is embedded in our lives like a mustard seed. Our overriding purpose is to grow with the spirit of the living God toward the remarkable destiny that awaits us.

We may not perceive much of our eternal destiny during our lifetimes, but we can perceive our individual call, and that may be all we really need to know. A vast, immeasurable cosmos may feel intimidating and overwhelming to us. Yet there is a way within it that is responsive and intimately personal. That way—the way of the spirit and its breath of pure joy—is available to each of us.

"Trust God and love others." That ancient and timeless message echoes through the millennia. Follow your joy. Love generously. The best is yet to come.

At the darkest moment comes the light.

Joseph Campbell

Man, it seems, is tempted—perhaps we should say "invited"—to fall; invited, it seems, by God Himself. Through this fall a certain definite struggle is offered to man. If he refuses this struggle, he dies. If he accepts this struggle, he is brought to a destiny so exalted that—as it is sometimes said—even the angels in heaven bow down before him.

Jacob Needleman

We keep our pictures of God secret from each other and often even from ourselves. For what would others think if we talked of God as a stalking animal, sniffing us like prey, or as an alien, a foreigner whose breath is upon our face, or whose foot is on our neck?

Ann Belford Ulanov

One must respond to one's fate or one's destiny or pay a heavy price. One must yield to it; one must surrender to it. One must permit oneself to be chosen.

Abraham Maslow

Do not search in distant skies for God. In man's own heart is He found.

Shinto passage

Death is not the greatest loss in life; the greatest loss is what dies inside us while we live.

Norman Cousins

The biggest human temptation is to settle for too little.

Thomas Merton

I have learned, as a rule of thumb, never to ask whether you can do something. Say, instead, that you are doing it. Then fasten your seat belt. The most remarkable things follow.

Julia Cameron

Just don't give up trying to do what you really want to do. Where there's love and inspiration, I don't think you can go wrong.

Ella Fitzgerald

I am only one; but still I am one. I cannot do everything, but still I can do something. I will not refuse to do the something I can do.

Helen Keller

"What is life's heaviest burden?" asked the child. "To have nothing to carry," answered the old man.

Anonymous

In dreams begin our possibilities.

William Shakespeare

One can never consent to creep when one feels the impulse to soar.

Helen Keller

It is only with the heart that one can see rightly; what is essential is invisible to the eye.

Antoine de Saint Exupery

What lies behind us and what lies before us are tiny matters, compared to what lies within us.

Ralph Waldo Emerson

As long as you have not grasped that you have to die to grow, you are a troubled guest on the dark earth.

Goethe

You gain strength, courage and confidence by every experience in which you really stop to look fear in the face . . . You must do the thing which you think you cannot do.

Eleanor Roosevelt

Let us be of good cheer, remembering that the misfortunes hardest to bear are those that never come.

Amy Lowell

I will tell you that there have been no failures in my life
. . . There have been some tremendous lessons.

Oprah Winfrey

Those who love deeply never grow old; they may die of old age, but they die young.

Benjamin Franklin

That love is all there is, is all we know of love.

Emily Dickinson

Love justice; do kindness; walk humbly with God.

Micah

Trust in the Lord and he will grant your heart's desire.

Psalm 37

About the Author

James Graham Johnston is founder of Gifts Compass Incorporated and the architect of the *GiftsCompass™ Inventory*, an online instrument that helps people orient to their best gifts.

James has formal educational training in fine art, architecture, and business. He has also pursued a lifelong interest in philosophy, psychology, and religion. To reach the author, please use his email address: jgjohnston@GiftsCompass.com

Gifts Compass Inc. is dedicated to providing resources to people for a well-lived life.

Among those resources is the online self-assessment, the *GiftsCompass Inventory* (GCI). Based on Carl Jung's psychological types, the GCI helps to clarify personal aptitudes and provides guidance for living a uniquely authentic life. To learn more, please visit www.GiftsCompass.com

Made in the USA
Charleston, SC
23 April 2010